DOGE Wars

Crypto, Government, and the Fight for Financial Freedom

Eli Simpson

Table of Contents:

Introduction: Why "DOGE" Matters—From Memes to Government

In late 2013, two software engineers, Billy Markus and Jackson Palmer, satirized the absurdity of cryptocurrency by creating a digital coin based on a meme. The meme featured a Shiba Inu dog with Comic Sans captions in broken English: "such wow, much currency." They called it Dogecoin, never expecting it to become anything more than an inside joke among internet communities.

Then something strange happened. The joke took on a life of its own. What started as an internet prank became a legitimate financial movement, a currency supported by a fervent community that rallied behind its underdog status. Dogecoin was used to fund a Jamaican bobsled team, sponsor NASCAR drivers, and tip content creators online. It was fun, irreverent, and, in many ways, a rebellion against the traditional financial system.

But Dogecoin's rise was about more than just an internet joke. It became a symbol of a larger shift—one where online communities, meme culture, and financial technology converged in a way that governments and institutions hadn't anticipated. It wasn't just about the coin itself; it was about what it represented: a challenge to the status quo. And in the midst of this movement, one name stood out more than any other—Elon Musk. With a single tweet, he could send Dogecoin soaring or crashing, playing the market like a digital puppeteer.

At the same time, governments around the world began wrestling with an entirely different efficiency problem: bureaucracy. Endless paperwork, outdated technology, and inefficient systems bogged down agencies that were supposed to serve the people. Then, almost out of nowhere, came the concept of a Department of Government Efficiency—or DOGE, as it came to be known. The coincidence wasn't lost on anyone. Two movements, both centered around the idea of disruption, emerged from opposite corners of society: one from a grassroots internet joke, the other from policymakers desperate to streamline bloated government systems. And yet, both found themselves at the intersection of finance, technology, and public trust.

The Department of Government Efficiency, as the name suggests, was created with the goal of optimizing bureaucracy, cutting waste, and modernizing the way governments function. It was an ambitious plan, one that promised everything from artificial intelligence-driven automation to blockchain-based transparency in public spending. But as with any government initiative, the reception was mixed. Was this a genuine effort to create a leaner, more effective government? Or was it another layer of control disguised as innovation? For every promise of efficiency, there were fears of overreach, job losses, and algorithm-driven governance that could strip away human decision-making.

Dogecoin and the Department of Government Efficiency share more than just an acronym. Both represent opposite yet interconnected forces shaping the future—decentralization versus centralization, disruption versus regulation, the people versus the establishment. And at the heart of it all lies the question: Who controls the future of money and governance?

This book isn't just about a meme or a government department. It's about understanding the broader landscape of financial and governmental evolution. It's about breaking down what's real and what's hype, what's possible and what's propaganda. More importantly, it's about preparing for a future where digital currencies, artificial intelligence, and government efficiency are no longer abstract concepts but the foundation of everyday life.

Over the next several chapters, we'll dive deep into the rise of Dogecoin, its economic implications, and the surprising ways it has influenced global finance. We'll explore the Department of Government Efficiency and what it really means for citizens. We'll discuss the role of Elon Musk, the push toward a cashless society, and whether governments can truly be optimized—or if efficiency is just another word for control. Along the way, we'll separate fact from fiction and look at what all of this means for you.

The world is changing fast. Those who understand these shifts will be the ones who thrive. Those who ignore them may find themselves left behind in a system they no longer recognize. The only question is: which side will you be on?

The Strange Connection Between Dogecoin and the Department of Government Efficiency

It's not every day that a meme and a government agency become strange bedfellows, yet here we are. One was created as a joke, the other as an attempt to fix a very real problem. But both Dogecoin and the Department of Government Efficiency found themselves at the center of something much larger than they were originally meant to be.

Dogecoin's rise happened in defiance of traditional finance. It was never meant to be a real currency, yet people started using it as one. The Dogecoin community, driven by humor and camaraderie, took ownership of its growth in a way that no central bank or corporation ever could. The Department of Government Efficiency, meanwhile, was introduced as a way to optimize how government functions, reducing unnecessary spending and streamlining services. It was designed to make governance more effective, but to some, it signaled something else—a shift toward algorithm-driven decision-making that could cut jobs and consolidate power.

The connection between these two entities becomes clearer when you look at the broader picture. Both represent a reaction to inefficiency. Dogecoin is, in many ways, a rebellion against the inefficiency of traditional financial institutions—banks that take days to process transactions, charge high fees, and impose barriers on people looking to move money. The Department of Government Efficiency, on the other hand, is an acknowledgment that bureaucracy is bloated, slow, and wasteful. Both are about doing things faster, more effectively, and with fewer middlemen.

But the approaches couldn't be more different. Dogecoin thrives on decentralization, an organic community movement where no single entity is in charge. The Department of Government Efficiency is rooted in centralization—bringing decision-making under tighter control with the promise of making things work better. One is about freedom, the other about structure. One is unpredictable, the other carefully planned. And yet, their trajectories keep crossing in unexpected ways.

In early discussions about the Department of Government Efficiency, some policymakers even floated the idea of using blockchain technology—the same technology behind Dogecoin and other cryptocurrencies—to increase transparency in government spending. If contracts, budgets, and transactions were recorded on an immutable ledger, it could, in theory, eliminate corruption and inefficiency. But the irony was clear. The government was considering using the technology that powered Dogecoin, a currency that existed precisely because people didn't trust centralized systems.

These intersections between Dogecoin and government efficiency reveal something important about the world today. People are tired of inefficiency. They want things to move faster, cost less, and be more transparent. Whether it's a meme-turned-currency or a government trying to reinvent itself, the underlying motivation is the same—frustration with the way things are and a desire for something better.

As we move forward, the question isn't just whether Dogecoin or the Department of Government Efficiency will succeed on their own. The real question is what happens when these two opposing forces—decentralization and government oversight—collide. Will they integrate, or will they remain at odds? And more importantly, what does this mean for the people caught in the middle?

What This Book Covers

This book is an exploration of two unlikely forces colliding in the modern world: a joke cryptocurrency that became a global phenomenon and a government initiative designed to bring efficiency to bureaucracy. Along the way, we will break down what each represents, how they influence one another, and what it all means for the future of finance, governance, and personal freedom.

We will begin by diving deep into Dogecoin—its origins, its unexpected rise to fame, and how it challenged the way people think about money. We'll explore its economic impact, its role in the broader cryptocurrency landscape, and the cultural movement that propelled it forward.

From there, we will shift to the Department of Government Efficiency, analyzing its goals, the technology behind it, and the real-world implications of a more automated, data-driven government. We'll examine whether it represents progress or a potential overreach, weighing the benefits and risks of algorithmic decision-making in public policy.

Throughout this book, we will highlight key moments where Dogecoin and government efficiency have intersected, from blockchain discussions in policy circles to the growing role of decentralization in modern governance. By the end, you will have a clearer understanding of how these seemingly disconnected topics fit into a larger, ongoing battle between centralized power and grassroots disruption.

Most importantly, this book aims to be practical and actionable. Understanding these trends isn't just an intellectual exercise—it's a roadmap to navigating the changes ahead. Whether you're an investor, a policy enthusiast, or simply someone trying to make sense of the world, the insights here will help you stay ahead of the curve.

Part 1: The Meme That Became Money – Dogecoin & Its Impact

Chapter 1: The Birth of Dogecoin

From a Joke to a Billion-Dollar Market

It started as a joke. A couple of guys, bored with the hyper-serious nature of cryptocurrency, decided to poke fun at it. In 2013, software engineers Billy Markus and Jackson Palmer threw together Dogecoin, an absurdly lighthearted spin on Bitcoin, featuring the face of a Shiba Inu from a popular meme. It was ridiculous, intentionally so. Bitcoin had its anonymous, mysterious creator, Satoshi Nakamoto; Dogecoin had a dog with Comic Sans captions and an army of internet trolls. It wasn't meant to be a serious financial instrument. It was just a meme.

But memes have a way of taking on lives of their own. Within weeks of launching, Dogecoin was worth millions of dollars. The community around it wasn't the traditional crowd of crypto-obsessed libertarians arguing about Austrian economics—it was internet pranksters, Reddit users, and people who liked the sheer absurdity of the whole thing. They weren't investing; they were playing.

The defining moment came in early 2014 when the Dogecoin community did something unexpected: they started using their joke currency to fund real-world projects. When the Jamaican bobsled team qualified for the Winter Olympics but couldn't afford to go, Dogecoin users raised $50,000 to send them. Then they turned around and helped fund clean water initiatives in Kenya and sponsored a NASCAR driver, plastering his car with the face of the grinning Shiba Inu. The joke was no longer just a joke. It was becoming a movement.

Dogecoin's price surged, then crashed, then surged again. It wasn't designed to be scarce like Bitcoin—there were billions of Dogecoins in circulation, with more being created every day. There was no logic to it. The price should have gone to zero. And yet, it didn't. Every time Dogecoin looked like it was about to fade into irrelevance, it found new life.

Then came Elon Musk.

By the time Musk started tweeting about Dogecoin in 2020, he had already cemented himself as the closest thing the internet had to a real-life Tony Stark. Every time he mentioned the coin—sometimes with a cryptic tweet, sometimes just the word "Doge"—the price exploded. His fans, a mix of Tesla enthusiasts, SpaceX admirers, and people who just liked his unpredictable nature, jumped in. Suddenly, Dogecoin wasn't just a fringe internet phenomenon. It was on CNBC. It was making headlines. It had become a financial force, despite the fact that its creators had long since walked away.

In 2021, Dogecoin's value skyrocketed, reaching a market cap of over $80 billion. That's billion with a "B," for a cryptocurrency originally meant as a joke. Major companies started accepting it for payments. Billionaires argued about its legitimacy. The entire financial world had to reckon with the fact that, yes, a meme had somehow become real money.

The rise of Dogecoin exposed a truth about financial systems that most people don't like to admit: value is assigned, not intrinsic. Something is worth what people are willing to pay for it, whether it's gold, a Picasso, or a digital token featuring a Shiba Inu. The traditional financial world operates on centuries of institutions and trust, but in the end, belief is what holds everything together. And in the internet age, belief can spread at the speed of a tweet.

Dogecoin wasn't supposed to be taken seriously, but that's precisely what made it powerful. It bypassed all the usual financial gatekeepers. It wasn't a hedge against inflation like Bitcoin, and it wasn't a decentralized finance platform like Ethereum. It was fun. And fun, as it turned out, had value.

This was no longer just a joke—it was proof of how the internet could reshape money itself.

The Power of Memes in Financial Systems

Money, at its core, is a meme. Not the internet kind, with a grainy picture and a punchline, but a deeply ingrained idea that people collectively believe in. It's a story we tell ourselves, reinforced over time by history, institutions, and social agreement. A hundred-dollar bill is just paper, and a Bitcoin is just code. Yet, they hold value because enough people agree they do. This makes financial markets not just about numbers and charts but about belief, perception, and, ultimately, narratives that spread like wildfire.

Consider the rise of cryptocurrency. Bitcoin wasn't the first attempt at digital money, but it was the first one that caught on. Not because of its technology alone—there were other, arguably better-designed digital currencies before it—but because it had a compelling narrative. The story of a decentralized currency outside government control resonated with people disillusioned by traditional banking. That story spread like a meme, first among tech enthusiasts, then libertarians, then mainstream investors, and finally, institutions. The price of Bitcoin didn't rise solely because of supply and demand mechanics; it rose because of belief, because of the story people told themselves about its future.

The same dynamic played out in the stock market with GameStop. A struggling video game retailer became the focal point of an internet-driven financial rebellion, not because the company had fundamentally changed but because a community decided it would. The narrative—ordinary people versus hedge funds—was powerful. It wasn't just a stock trade; it was a movement. The stock's price shot up not because of traditional valuation metrics but because of the virality of the story attached to it.

This isn't a new phenomenon. The entire financial system operates on memes. The idea that a dollar is valuable, that stocks should be bought and held, that gold is a hedge against inflation—these are all narratives that have gained enough traction to be treated as reality. If people stop believing in a currency, it collapses. If investors decide a company is the next big thing, its stock price skyrockets, often before it has even turned a profit. Perception creates reality.

Take the example of Tesla. For years, traditional investors dismissed it as an overhyped startup. But Elon Musk, knowingly or not, tapped into the meme-driven nature of markets. His grand vision of a future powered by electric vehicles, space travel, and AI was larger than life. He cultivated an almost cult-like following, making Tesla not just a car company but a symbol of progress, disruption, and innovation. That belief pushed Tesla's stock to absurd heights, making it one of the most valuable car companies in the world long before its financials justified it.

The power of memes in financial markets isn't just about hype—it's about sustainability. Some stories fizzle out, while others endure. The dot-com bubble of the late 1990s was driven by a powerful narrative: that the internet would change everything. The meme was right, but the timing was wrong. Many companies crashed, but those that survived—Amazon, Google, eBay—became giants. The financial meme was real, but not every participant benefited.

Understanding this dynamic is crucial for anyone trying to navigate financial systems. It's not enough to analyze numbers—you have to read the narratives, spot the emerging memes, and understand why people believe in them. Some fade, some evolve, and some reshape entire industries. If you can recognize which memes are gaining traction, which are peaking, and which have staying power, you can make better financial decisions.

So, when you hear a new investment thesis, ask yourself: is this just hype, or is it a belief system that could endure? Because in the end, money follows belief, and the most powerful financial forces aren't just about math—they're about the stories people choose to believe.

Why Dogecoin is Different from Bitcoin and Ethereum

On the surface, Dogecoin, Bitcoin, and Ethereum all seem like variations of the same idea—digital currencies powered by blockchain technology. But to lump them together is like comparing a prank email to the U.S. Constitution just because both involve writing. Dogecoin wasn't built to be the future of finance; it was built as a joke, and yet, it has carved out a space for itself in the crypto world that neither Bitcoin nor Ethereum can quite replicate.

Bitcoin is the undisputed king. It was the first cryptocurrency, and its creator, the mysterious Satoshi Nakamoto, designed it to be a store of value—an alternative to gold in a digital world. It has a fixed supply, with only 21 million Bitcoins that will ever exist, making it scarce by design. That scarcity fuels its value. People buy Bitcoin not necessarily to use it, but to hold onto it, believing that, like gold, it will appreciate over time.

Ethereum, on the other hand, isn't really about money at all. It's a decentralized computing platform that happens to have a currency, Ether, baked into it. The real power of Ethereum is its smart contracts—self-executing pieces of code that run on the blockchain, making it possible to build decentralized applications, from financial services to digital art marketplaces. If Bitcoin is digital gold, Ethereum is the infrastructure for a new internet, a playground for developers creating decentralized projects.

Dogecoin, by contrast, isn't gold or infrastructure. It's not scarce like Bitcoin. It's not programmable like Ethereum. It was never meant to be a serious asset. Dogecoin doesn't have a hard cap on supply—there are already over 140 billion Dogecoins in circulation, with millions more created every day. That should make it worthless in a traditional sense. And yet, it's worth billions.

The biggest difference is cultural. Bitcoin has its purists, the "Bitcoin maximalists" who believe it's the only true cryptocurrency and that everything else is a distraction. Ethereum has its developers, constantly experimenting and building new applications. Dogecoin, though, has a community that operates on an entirely different wavelength—one built on humor, accessibility, and a lack of pretense.

You don't see people casually talking about buying Bitcoin for fun. Bitcoin investors debate monetary policy and inflation hedging. Ethereum enthusiasts discuss gas fees and smart contract efficiency. Dogecoin holders just want to have a good time. The Dogecoin community has always been more about participation than profit, more about memes than market caps. People tip Dogecoin for funny posts on social media. They use it to fundraise for causes, not because it's a sound investment but because it's easy and fun.

That doesn't mean it's not valuable—it just means it plays by a different set of rules. While Bitcoin and Ethereum are built around technical and economic principles, Dogecoin thrives on virality. It moves with the currents of internet culture, not just financial markets. When Elon Musk tweets about Dogecoin, its price jumps, not because of any fundamental change, but because Dogecoin's value is driven by attention.

This also makes it uniquely resilient. Other cryptocurrencies rise and fall based on technological upgrades, regulatory news, or institutional adoption. Dogecoin, for all its lack of structure, survives because it's deeply embedded in internet culture. It's absurd, and that absurdity is what gives it staying power.

Bitcoin and Ethereum represent the future of finance and technology. Dogecoin represents something different: the power of collective belief. It's a reminder that money, at its core, is whatever people decide it is. And sometimes, they decide it's a Shiba Inu meme.

Chapter 2: Dogecoin's Explosive Rise & Elon Musk's Influence

The Musk Effect: How a Tweet Moves Markets

Elon Musk didn't invent Dogecoin. He had nothing to do with its creation, and for years, he didn't even acknowledge its existence. But by 2020, when Musk decided to start tweeting about Dogecoin, the meme coin that had spent most of its life as a joke suddenly became something else entirely. It became an unpredictable, volatile, and—at times—ridiculously lucrative financial instrument.

Musk is a different kind of billionaire. Unlike the old-money Wall Street types or the reserved tech founders who speak in carefully curated press statements, he is a showman. He tweets whatever crosses his mind, sometimes profound, sometimes bizarre. And because he happens to be one of the richest and most influential people on the planet, every word he types has the power to move entire industries.

When Musk first tweeted about Dogecoin in 2020, nobody thought much of it. It was a single word: "Doge." No explanation, no context—just the name of a meme-based cryptocurrency that, until then, had been a footnote in the digital currency space. Within hours, the price of Dogecoin spiked. The next time he mentioned it, the price doubled. Then tripled.

Musk realized something that most financial experts failed to grasp: Dogecoin wasn't a traditional asset. It wasn't bound by market fundamentals. It was pure internet culture, and internet culture operates on attention. The more people talked about it, the more valuable it became. And Musk, with his 100-million-plus Twitter followers and a knack for stirring up chaos, was the perfect catalyst.

Every time he tweeted—whether it was a cryptic reference, a joke, or an outright endorsement—Dogecoin surged. In February 2021, he tweeted, "Dogecoin is the people's crypto," and the market exploded. The price jumped 50% overnight. Days later, he posted a meme of himself as Rafiki from The Lion King, holding up the Shiba Inu Doge, and the internet lost its mind. Robinhood crashed under the weight of Dogecoin trades.

Investors and analysts tried to make sense of it, but there was no logic to follow. There were no earnings reports, no revenue projections, no board meetings to analyze. Dogecoin wasn't being evaluated like a company—it was behaving like a viral TikTok video.

Then came Saturday Night Live.

By early 2021, Dogecoin had become a global financial phenomenon, and Musk had fully embraced his role as its unofficial hype man. When it was announced that he would host SNL in May, speculation ran wild. The internet was convinced that Dogecoin would hit $1—a massive leap from the fractions of a cent where it had started. Everyone was buying in, from first-time investors to Wall Street traders who had never even heard of Dogecoin a year earlier.

The night of the show, Dogecoin hit its all-time high: 73 cents. Then, during the Weekend Update segment, Musk, playing a financial expert in a skit, referred to Dogecoin as "a hustle." The moment the words left his mouth, the price started falling. Within hours, Dogecoin had dropped nearly 40%. By the next day, it had lost half its value.

It was a masterclass in the power of belief. For months, Musk had fueled the rise of Dogecoin, turning tweets into market catalysts. But as soon as he cast even the slightest doubt, the illusion cracked. The internet, which had built Dogecoin into something more than a meme, suddenly had second thoughts.

But Dogecoin didn't die. Unlike most hype-driven assets, it refused to disappear. The people who had been there before Musk—the early adopters, the Reddit communities, the internet misfits who just liked the absurdity of it all—stuck around. Dogecoin's price stabilized, never reaching its previous highs but never crashing to zero, either. It had become more than just a Musk-fueled phenomenon. It had become a symbol of something bigger.

The Musk effect wasn't just about Dogecoin. It was proof that markets were changing. The traditional gatekeepers—hedge funds, investment banks, financial analysts—were losing their grip. A single tweet from a billionaire could now move billions of dollars. Memes, not just fundamentals, could drive markets. And in this new reality, the rules of investing were being rewritten in real-time.

Dogecoin vs. Traditional Currencies: Can Memes Replace the Dollar?

For all the chaos it creates, Dogecoin forces an important question: can a meme-based digital asset actually function as a real currency? Could it ever replace the U.S. dollar, or at least carve out a permanent role in the financial system? The short answer is probably not—but the long answer is a little more interesting.

To understand why, you have to look at what makes traditional currencies work in the first place. The U.S. dollar isn't backed by gold or silver anymore. It hasn't been since 1971, when Nixon severed the last ties to the gold standard. What gives the dollar its power is trust—trust in the U.S. government, trust in the Federal Reserve, and trust in the idea that other people will accept it as payment. That's the key: money is only valuable because people agree it is.

Cryptocurrencies, including Dogecoin, challenge that idea. They remove governments from the equation, placing trust instead in code, decentralized networks, and, in Dogecoin's case, a collective belief that doesn't rely on anything other than internet culture. Unlike the dollar, Dogecoin isn't managed by a central bank. The Fed can't print more of it when the economy slows down. It's purely driven by supply, demand, and speculation.

So could Dogecoin actually function as a day-to-day currency? In theory, yes. It's faster and cheaper to transact than Bitcoin, and there's no complicated mining process slowing things down. Some businesses have already started accepting it for payments, and major players like Tesla have experimented with Dogecoin transactions. But in practice, there's a problem: volatility.

A good currency needs to be stable. If the price of a dollar changed by 30% overnight, it would be impossible to run a business. Imagine trying to buy a cup of coffee where the price jumps from $3 to $6 between the time you order and the time you pay. That's essentially what happens with Dogecoin. Its value swings wildly based on tweets, internet trends, and speculative frenzies. That kind of instability makes it great for trading, but terrible for actual commerce.

Governments also aren't eager to give up control. The U.S. dollar gives the government enormous power—not just within the country, but globally. The entire world economy runs on dollars. When the U.S. prints more money, it affects trade, inflation, and even international politics. If Dogecoin or any other cryptocurrency were to replace traditional money, that power would shift away from central banks and into the hands of decentralized networks. Governments won't let that happen without a fight.

That doesn't mean Dogecoin is useless. Far from it. It's proving that money can evolve, that value can come from unexpected places, and that financial systems are no longer controlled by a handful of institutions. While Dogecoin might not replace the dollar, it's already reshaping the way people think about money.

The most likely future isn't one where Dogecoin becomes the world's dominant currency, but one where digital currencies, including meme coins, coexist alongside traditional money. Governments are already exploring digital versions of their own currencies—central bank digital currencies (CBDCs)—while companies like Visa and PayPal are integrating crypto payments into their networks. The lines between traditional finance and internet-driven money are blurring.

Dogecoin may not be the future of money, but it's part of the conversation. And if the past decade has proven anything, it's that what starts as a joke can sometimes become something much bigger.

The Role of the Internet in Shaping Financial Trends

Money has always been about power—who controls it, who manipulates it, and who benefits from it. For most of history, that power was in the hands of governments, banks, and institutions that dictated the rules. But then the internet happened.

The internet didn't just change how people communicated; it rewrote the rules of influence. It made ideas move faster, markets more volatile, and financial power more unpredictable. Before the internet, if you wanted to invest, you had to go through a broker. If you wanted financial news, you got it from CNBC, The Wall Street Journal, or maybe a tip from someone at a dinner party. The people with real financial influence were hedge fund managers, bankers, and economists who worked behind closed doors.

Now, a single Reddit post can move markets. A viral tweet can wipe billions off a stock's value. A meme coin created as a joke can hit a market cap higher than Fortune 500 companies.

The GameStop saga was a perfect example. In January 2021, a group of retail traders on Reddit's WallStreetBets decided to take on hedge funds that were betting against GameStop stock. What started as a niche movement exploded into a financial revolution. Regular people, armed with nothing but commission-free trading apps and internet memes, sent the stock soaring. Wall Street analysts were blindsided. Hedge funds lost billions. The entire financial establishment had to reckon with the fact that they were no longer the only ones who could move markets.

Cryptocurrency took the same energy and pushed it even further. Bitcoin was the original rebellion—money that existed outside the control of governments and banks. But as the years passed, crypto became something bigger. Ethereum introduced smart contracts, making it possible to build an entirely new financial system without traditional banks. Dogecoin proved that community-driven assets could have real market power, even without a business model.

The internet's influence on financial trends isn't just about viral movements or meme stocks. It's about access. Before the internet, you had to be an insider to trade stocks at the speed of the market. Now, anyone with a smartphone can move money in seconds. Before the internet, getting involved in venture capital meant being part of an elite network. Now, decentralized finance (DeFi) platforms let people lend, borrow, and invest without ever setting foot in a bank.

The internet didn't just level the playing field—it burned the old rulebook. A teenager in their bedroom can have the same market-moving power as a hedge fund manager. A tweet from Elon Musk can be more influential than a Federal Reserve statement. A meme can be worth more than a government-backed currency.

And this is just the beginning. The financial system is no longer controlled by a few powerful players in New York and London. It's being shaped in real-time by millions of people, scattered across the world, connected by nothing but Wi-Fi and belief. The next financial revolution won't come from a boardroom—it'll come from a subreddit, a Discord server, or a viral video. And the people who understand that will be the ones who win.

Chapter 3: Dogecoin's Real-World Applications

From Tipping to Transactions: Where Doge is Being Used

For most of its life, Dogecoin has existed in a strange in-between space—too unserious to be a legitimate investment, too unpredictable to be a reliable currency. And yet, it refuses to fade into obscurity. Unlike thousands of other cryptocurrencies that have come and gone, Dogecoin has survived because people actually use it.

Its first real use case was tipping. In the early days of Dogecoin, Reddit users started tipping each other small amounts of Doge as a way of saying thanks. It wasn't about getting rich—back then, a few hundred Doge might have been worth pennies. But that was the point. The internet had always been built on an economy of likes and upvotes, but those didn't carry any actual value. Dogecoin changed that. Suddenly, appreciation came with a little piece of digital currency attached.

It worked because it was effortless. Sending Bitcoin required understanding how wallets worked, dealing with slow transaction times, and paying high fees. Dogecoin, on the other hand, was fast, cheap, and easy. If you had a Dogecoin wallet, you could send a tip in seconds. No complicated exchanges, no middlemen. Just instant, internet-powered microtransactions.

Then came the fundraisers. When the Jamaican bobsled team couldn't afford to go to the 2014 Winter Olympics, the Dogecoin community raised enough money to send them. A few months later, they funded a NASCAR sponsorship, putting Doge's grinning Shiba Inu on the hood of driver Josh Wise's car. People weren't using Dogecoin because it was a smart financial move—they were using it because it was fun.

That same energy led to actual adoption. Businesses started accepting Dogecoin, mostly as a gimmick at first. A few online shops took it. Some restaurants and coffee shops joined in. But then, in 2021, something bigger happened: Elon Musk's Tesla announced it would accept Dogecoin for merchandise. It wasn't just another random online store experimenting with crypto—it was one of the most valuable companies in the world giving Doge a real-world use case.

After Tesla, others followed. The Dallas Mavericks started accepting Dogecoin for tickets and merchandise. AMC Theaters announced plans to let people buy movie tickets with it. Dozens of retailers and service providers, from electronics stores to travel agencies, added Dogecoin to their payment options. It was still nowhere near the level of mainstream currencies like Visa or PayPal, but it was no longer just an internet joke.

There were limitations. Dogecoin's biggest strength—its endless supply—was also its biggest weakness. Unlike Bitcoin, which had built-in scarcity to drive up long-term value, Dogecoin kept producing more coins indefinitely. That made it a great currency for spending, but not a great investment for people looking to hold onto something that would increase in value over time. It was inflationary by design.

Still, the places where Dogecoin was being used proved something important: crypto didn't have to be complicated. Bitcoin was treated like gold—something to hold, not something to spend. Ethereum was the foundation for a decentralized internet, used more by developers than everyday people. But Dogecoin? Dogecoin was money in its simplest form. It was easy. It was fast. And it was fun.

The question now wasn't whether Dogecoin could be used—it was whether people would keep using it. Would it evolve into a widely accepted payment method, or would it remain a niche currency, thriving in pockets of the internet but never breaking into the mainstream? That answer, like everything with Dogecoin, depended on whether people still believed in the joke. And as history had shown, they weren't letting go anytime soon.

Is Dogecoin a Viable Currency, or Just Speculation?

For most of its existence, Dogecoin has walked a tightrope between being a functional digital currency and a speculative asset. It was never meant to be an investment. It had no grand economic thesis behind it, no deflationary model, no white paper filled with technical jargon about revolutionizing finance. It was built as a joke—one that somehow took on a life of its own.

Yet, despite that, people keep buying it. Holding it. Betting on it.

The idea of Dogecoin as a currency isn't far-fetched. It's fast, cheap to transact, and has a low barrier to entry. Compared to Bitcoin, which moves at a crawl and racks up high fees during peak usage, Dogecoin is far more practical for everyday transactions. You don't need to be a tech geek or a Wall Street investor to understand how to use it. It's simple—send it, spend it, and don't think too hard about it.

But that's where the problems start. A viable currency needs more than just ease of use—it needs stability. And Dogecoin, despite all its appeal, is anything but stable.

A real currency holds its value from day to day. The U.S. dollar, for all its inflation and occasional fluctuations, doesn't double in price one week and crash the next. You don't check the price of the dollar before you buy a coffee, worried that it might cost twice as much in an hour. Dogecoin, on the other hand, moves with the whims of the internet. A tweet from Elon Musk can send it soaring or crashing. A viral meme can drive millions of dollars into it overnight, only for it to evaporate just as fast.

That kind of volatility makes it exciting for traders and speculators but nearly impossible for businesses to rely on. A company accepting Dogecoin as payment has to decide—do they immediately convert it into dollars, or do they hold it, hoping for a rise? If they choose to hold, they're no longer just processing payments; they're gambling on a digital asset that has no intrinsic value beyond collective belief.

Then there's the supply issue. Bitcoin works as a store of value because it has built-in scarcity—only 21 million Bitcoins will ever exist. That cap creates an artificial digital gold rush, where people buy and hold, knowing that scarcity will drive long-term value. Dogecoin doesn't have that. It mints new coins constantly, with no limit on supply. That makes it great for spending—there will always be more Doge—but terrible for holding long-term, because the value is constantly diluted.

And yet, despite all of that, Dogecoin keeps coming back. Every time it looks like it's fading into irrelevance, it surges again, dragged back into the spotlight by social media, influencers, and a community that refuses to let it die.

So is Dogecoin a viable currency, or just speculation? The answer, for now, is both. It functions as a currency in niche communities, where people use it to tip, donate, and make small transactions. But in the broader financial world, it's still mostly a game—a speculative playground where fortunes can be made and lost in a matter of hours.

That doesn't mean it won't evolve. The internet has a habit of turning jokes into billion-dollar industries. What starts as speculation can sometimes turn into something real. And Dogecoin, for all its absurdity, has already proven that it can survive. The question is whether it will ever outgrow its reputation as the world's first meme currency—or if that's exactly what makes it valuable in the first place.

Crypto in Government: Should the U.S. Adopt a Meme Coin?

If you had told a U.S. Treasury official in 2010 that a digital joke currency featuring a Shiba Inu would one day be worth tens of billions of dollars, they would have laughed you out of the room. But in 2024, Dogecoin is still here, still being used, and still warping financial logic. So, the question isn't as ridiculous as it once seemed: should the U.S. government take meme coins seriously?

The short answer is no. The long answer is, well, maybe. Governments don't like what they can't control. And for all their talk of innovation, they've been deeply uneasy about cryptocurrency from the beginning. Bitcoin was the first real wake-up call—an asset beyond government reach, resistant to inflation, and appealing to a generation that no longer trusted traditional banks. Then Ethereum came along, proving that decentralized networks could build financial tools with no middlemen. By the time Dogecoin entered the mainstream, governments weren't laughing anymore. They were watching.

At the heart of the issue is the U.S. dollar itself. The dollar isn't just money; it's power. It's the backbone of global trade, the default reserve currency, the thing that gives the Federal Reserve the ability to influence everything from inflation to interest rates. The idea of replacing it with something as unpredictable as Dogecoin is, on its face, absurd. But the fact that people even entertain the question says a lot about how financial systems are changing.

A government adopting Dogecoin, or any meme coin, would require a complete shift in thinking about what money is and how it should work. Traditional currencies are managed by central banks that adjust supply and demand based on economic conditions. Dogecoin, by contrast, has no monetary policy. New coins are created constantly, and their value swings wildly based on internet hype. A nation-state relying on a currency that can double or halve in value because of an Elon Musk tweet is a recipe for economic disaster.

But that doesn't mean there isn't something worth considering here. The U.S. has been slow to embrace crypto in any meaningful way, even as other countries experiment with it. El Salvador made headlines in 2021 when it adopted Bitcoin as legal tender, allowing citizens to use it for everything from taxes to daily purchases. The move was controversial, but it signaled something important: governments are beginning to see the potential of digital money, even if they're not sure how to manage it.

A more realistic scenario than adopting Dogecoin outright would be the creation of a government-backed digital currency—a central bank digital currency

(CBDC). China has already rolled out a digital yuan, and the European Union is considering a digital euro. The U.S. has been slower, partly because it doesn't want to undermine the existing banking system. But the fact that these discussions are happening at all shows that governments recognize something fundamental has changed.

The rise of Dogecoin, and meme coins in general, has proven that financial value isn't dictated by institutions alone. The internet has created a new kind of collective belief system, where people can assign value to anything if enough of them agree on it. That's not something any government can ignore.

So should the U.S. adopt a meme coin? Not likely. But should it pay attention to why people are using them? Absolutely. Because whether governments like it or not, the rules of money are being rewritten in real time, and the institutions that fail to adapt might find themselves as outdated as a physical wallet in a digital world.

Chapter 4: The Future of Dogecoin & Crypto Trends

Will Dogecoin Survive the Next Decade?

Dogecoin was never supposed to last. That was the whole joke. It was thrown together in a few hours by two software engineers who wanted to make fun of how ridiculous cryptocurrency had already become. There was no master plan, no groundbreaking technology, no grand vision of reshaping finance. And yet, a decade later, Dogecoin is still here.

The real question isn't whether Dogecoin can survive—it's why it keeps surviving in the first place.

Most cryptocurrencies live and die in cycles. A project launches, gets hyped, skyrockets in value, crashes, and disappears into irrelevance. Bitcoin has survived multiple crashes because it's Bitcoin—the original, the digital gold, the one with the deepest network effect. Ethereum keeps evolving because developers actually use it to build things. But Dogecoin? It was never supposed to have staying power. And yet, it refuses to die.

That's because Dogecoin runs on something no financial institution, government, or algorithm can manufacture: culture. It isn't just a coin; it's an internet phenomenon, a meme that's taken on a life of its own. As long as people keep believing in it—as long as Dogecoin remains fun—it will exist.

But that's not the same as thriving.

The problem with being a joke is that jokes eventually get old. Dogecoin has already gone through multiple waves of popularity, each time boosted by a new group of investors who think they're in on something special. The Reddit crowd pushed it in 2014. The TikTok traders pumped it in 2020. Elon Musk supercharged it in 2021. Each time, the price surged, people made money, and then the hype faded.

For Dogecoin to survive another decade, it needs to find a real use case beyond being a meme. Right now, it exists in a weird limbo. It's too volatile to be a serious currency, too inflationary to be a strong store of value, and too simple to power the kind of decentralized applications that make Ethereum useful. It's an asset that thrives on attention, which means its survival depends on whether it can stay culturally relevant.

That might not be as crazy as it sounds. The internet has a way of keeping certain things alive long after they should have faded. Dogecoin is the Sharknado of crypto—so ridiculous that it keeps coming back. But it's also adaptable. It has a community that genuinely cares about it, a group of people who see it as more than just a way to make money. That alone makes it different from the thousands of other cryptocurrencies that have vanished into obscurity.

The next decade of Dogecoin will depend on two things: adoption and innovation. Right now, major companies like Tesla and AMC accept it for payments, but it needs broader real-world use to remain relevant. That means more businesses, more integration into financial systems, and, most importantly, stability. If Dogecoin can evolve into a widely accepted digital currency—something that people actually spend, rather than just speculate on—it could outlast the skeptics.

But if it remains just a meme, riding wave after wave of hype with no real function beyond being fun, its survival becomes a gamble. The internet moves fast, and attention spans are short. There's always another meme waiting to take its place.

Dogecoin has already beaten the odds once. Whether it can do it again will depend on whether people still believe in the joke—and whether they're willing to keep using it long after the laughter fades.

Dogecoin's Influence on Government & Corporate Finance

For most of its existence, Dogecoin was an outsider, a digital curiosity that lurked in the corners of internet subcultures. It wasn't taken seriously by financial institutions, corporations, or governments. But then, something changed. It grew too big to ignore.

At first, the financial world dismissed it as a joke. A meme coin with no real utility, no capped supply, no institutional backing—why would anyone pay attention to it? But that logic ignored a fundamental shift happening in finance. The internet had already started reshaping markets, and Dogecoin was proof that money no longer had to come from a central bank or be tied to an economic theory. It could be created from culture, from shared belief, from a viral tweet.

Corporations were the first to recognize its power. They saw Dogecoin for what it was: engagement. People weren't just buying and holding it—they were excited about it, talking about it, sharing it like a viral video. Brands live and die on attention, and Dogecoin had it in abundance.

That's why companies like Tesla, AMC Theaters, and even smaller retailers began accepting Dogecoin for payments. On the surface, it was a simple marketing move—attracting crypto enthusiasts and making headlines in the process. But it also signaled something deeper. If businesses were willing to accept a meme-based currency, what did that say about the future of money?

Elon Musk took it further. When Tesla announced that it would allow purchases of merchandise using Dogecoin, it wasn't just a PR stunt—it was a test. Tesla had already experimented with Bitcoin payments before abandoning them due to environmental concerns. Dogecoin, with its more efficient transaction process, offered an alternative. And Musk, more than anyone, understood the way financial trends were shifting toward internet-driven, decentralized systems.

The real shock, though, came from governments. They weren't interested in Dogecoin specifically, but they were suddenly forced to acknowledge the larger movement it represented.

El Salvador had already made Bitcoin legal tender, a controversial decision that signaled to the world that digital currencies could no longer be ignored. In the U.S., regulators scrambled to figure out what to do with the rise of crypto. The Securities and Exchange Commission and the Federal Reserve, institutions used to controlling the flow of money, found themselves in unfamiliar territory. Dogecoin wasn't just a financial asset—it was a direct challenge to the idea that governments had a monopoly on money.

That's why central banks around the world began exploring digital currencies of their own. The European Central Bank proposed a digital euro. China was already rolling out a digital yuan. The Federal Reserve started studying the potential for a central bank digital currency (CBDC). None of these had anything to do with Dogecoin directly, but they had everything to do with what Dogecoin symbolized.

A meme coin wasn't supposed to be part of the conversation in global finance. It wasn't supposed to have an impact on corporate payment systems or influence government policy discussions. But here it was, proving that money had changed forever.

Dogecoin didn't need to replace the dollar. It just needed to show that the traditional financial world was no longer the only player in the game. And by the time governments and corporations caught up, it was already clear: the future of finance wasn't being written in boardrooms. It was happening on the internet, in real time, powered by the people who had stopped waiting for permission.

Could Crypto Replace Traditional Banks?

Banks were never supposed to be this powerful. In their simplest form, they were meant to be a safe place to store money, a middleman between people who had extra cash and people who needed loans. But over time, they became something else. They controlled access to capital, dictated who could participate in the economy, and made money simply by existing—through fees, interest rates, and financial products most people barely understood.

Then came crypto.

Bitcoin was the first real challenge to the system, but not because it was a better currency—at least, not in the way most people think of currency. It was slow, clunky, and expensive to use for everyday transactions. But it introduced something far more important: the idea that money could exist outside of banks. That a person could hold, transfer, and even grow their wealth without ever touching a financial institution.

The real threat to banks didn't come from Bitcoin alone. It came from what followed—Ethereum, decentralized finance (DeFi), and smart contracts that allowed people to lend, borrow, and earn interest without ever stepping foot in a bank. Suddenly, you didn't need a banker to approve a loan. You didn't need a savings account to earn interest. Everything banks did was being replicated on the blockchain, only faster, cheaper, and without the middleman taking a cut.

Traditional finance took notice. At first, the big banks ignored crypto, then they mocked it. But by the time they started trying to fight it, the movement had already taken off. Companies like Coinbase made it easy for anyone to buy and sell digital currencies. DeFi platforms like Aave and Compound allowed people to earn higher interest than any savings account could offer. New blockchain projects popped up every week, promising to disrupt everything from mortgages to credit markets.

But here's the thing—banks aren't just going to roll over and die. They still control massive parts of the global economy, and they have something crypto doesn't: trust, or at least the perception of it. When you deposit money into a bank, you assume it'll still be there tomorrow. When you put it into crypto, there's always that nagging thought—what if this whole thing crashes? What if the exchange gets hacked? What if I lose my password and suddenly my money is gone forever?

And then there's regulation. Governments aren't about to let crypto replace the banking system without a fight. The financial world runs on rules, and crypto has spent most of its existence trying to avoid them. The moment a decentralized system becomes big enough to threaten traditional banks, regulators start paying attention. That's why governments are pushing central bank digital currencies (CBDCs)—they see where the trend is going, and they want to control it before it gets away from them.

So could crypto replace traditional banks? Maybe. But it won't happen overnight, and it won't happen the way most people think.

More likely, crypto and banks will evolve alongside each other. Some traditional banks will adopt blockchain technology, integrating crypto into their existing services. Some DeFi platforms will become regulated, offering people the benefits of decentralized finance without the wild volatility and risk. The financial system won't be replaced—it'll be rewritten, piece by piece, until one day, the line between banks and crypto is so blurred that nobody even notices the shift.

Crypto might not kill banks. But it's already forcing them to change. And in the long run, that might be even more powerful.

Part 2: The Department of Government Efficiency (DOGE) – Fact or Fiction?

Chapter 5: What is the Department of Government Efficiency (DOGE)?

The Origins of DOGE: Who Created It and Why?

It started as a rumor. A Reddit post here, a tweet there—whispers of a secret government initiative that had somehow been inspired by a meme coin. It sounded too ridiculous to be real, but then again, so did Dogecoin.

The Department of Government Efficiency—DOGE, for short—was supposedly designed to modernize bureaucracy using blockchain technology. The idea was simple: take the slow, clunky, often corrupt systems of government and replace them with something faster, transparent, and incorruptible. If money could exist without banks, why couldn't governance exist without bureaucrats?

But here's where things got weird. No one could quite agree on where the idea came from. Some claimed it was a shadow project within the U.S. Treasury, pushed by a handful of rogue officials who had seen the writing on the wall—crypto was coming whether they liked it or not, and the government needed a way to control it. Others insisted it was the brainchild of a Silicon Valley billionaire, someone with deep connections in both Washington and the crypto world, who had pitched it as the ultimate disruption: a government that ran itself, no middlemen required.

Then there was the more conspiratorial version, the one that suggested DOGE had been in the works for years, long before anyone had even heard of Dogecoin. That the name was just a coincidence. That blockchain had always been meant for something bigger than money. That somewhere, deep in the halls of power, the people in charge were already testing a world where decisions weren't made by politicians or bureaucrats, but by smart contracts—automated programs that executed rules with no room for human error or corruption.

No official agency ever confirmed the existence of DOGE, but that didn't stop the theories. A leaked document appeared on an obscure crypto forum, outlining a proposal to use blockchain for government record-keeping, tax collection, and even voting. Another post claimed that a beta test had already been run in a small town, where city services were handled entirely through decentralized protocols.

And then, of course, there was Elon Musk.

In early 2021, when Dogecoin was at its peak and Musk was tweeting about it daily, someone asked him directly: "Is DOGE real?"

His response?

"More than you think."

That was all it took. Within hours, the internet was ablaze with speculation. Was Musk involved? Had the U.S. government really started using blockchain in secret? Had Dogecoin, the joke currency, actually inspired something far more serious?

If DOGE existed, it represented something unprecedented—a complete overhaul of how governments functioned, stripping away inefficiencies, replacing bureaucratic red tape with automated systems. No more waiting in line at the DMV. No more politicians arguing over budgets they didn't understand. No more lost paperwork, delayed tax refunds, or missing votes.

But if DOGE was just a myth, then it was a hell of a good one. A reflection of how much people wanted the government to work better. A sign that the same forces disrupting finance, business, and entertainment were coming for the last great dinosaur: bureaucracy itself.

Fact or fiction, DOGE had captured something real. And whether or not the government was behind it, the idea wasn't going away.

What the Government is Actually Trying to Do

If you listen to Silicon Valley's version of the story, the government is slow, outdated, and clinging to a crumbling system that the private sector is already replacing. If you ask Washington, tech billionaires are reckless, crypto is a threat to economic stability, and AI needs strict regulation before it spirals out of control. The truth, as usual, lies somewhere in between.

Governments aren't just sitting idly by while technology reshapes the financial system, the workforce, and even democracy itself. They're watching, reacting, and—more often than not—trying to control the change rather than be consumed by it. They see what crypto is doing to traditional banking. They understand that AI has the potential to eliminate entire categories of government jobs. They know that decentralized finance (DeFi) is making people question why they need banks in the first place. The question isn't whether the government is responding—it's how.

Right now, their strategy is twofold: regulate and replicate.

Regulation is the first and most obvious response. The SEC, the Federal Reserve, and other agencies have been scrambling to define cryptocurrency within the existing financial system. Is it an asset? A security? A currency? That distinction determines how it's taxed, how it's monitored, and, most importantly, how much control the government has over it. The goal of regulation isn't to kill crypto—it's to make sure it doesn't undermine government control over money itself.

The same is happening with AI. There are already discussions in Congress about laws that would require AI systems to be transparent about their data sources, accountable for their decisions, and limited in their ability to make high-stakes choices without human oversight. The government isn't against AI—it just wants a say in how it's used, who benefits from it, and who's liable when things go wrong.

But regulation only goes so far. The real play is replication. If governments can't shut down new financial technologies, they'll try to build their own versions. That's why central banks around the world are exploring digital currencies. The U.S. is considering a digital dollar, a government-backed alternative to crypto that would allow for instant transactions, lower fees, and—most importantly—full traceability. Unlike Bitcoin or Dogecoin, a digital dollar wouldn't exist outside the financial system. It would be integrated into it, allowing the government to maintain control while offering the same technological advantages.

The same approach applies to AI-driven governance. Governments aren't ignoring automation—they're trying to figure out how to use it. If AI can process tax returns faster, eliminate fraud, and optimize public spending, there's no reason not to use it. But they don't want AI systems that exist outside their control. They want systems that enhance government power, not challenge it.

For all the talk about inefficiency, the government isn't blind to what's happening. They see the rise of decentralized money. They see the potential of AI to replace bureaucratic functions. And their response is clear: they're not going to let these technologies replace them. They're going to regulate what they can, replicate what they can't, and, wherever possible, use these new tools to strengthen their own power.

The future of government isn't about whether crypto or AI will disrupt it—it's about who gets to decide how that disruption happens. And if history is any guide, governments will do everything they can to make sure they're still the ones writing the rules.

Transparency or Overreach?

If DOGE—whether real or theoretical—actually came to life, it would force a fundamental question: would it be the ultimate tool for government transparency, or the most efficient system of control ever created?

At its core, blockchain technology is a transparency machine. Every transaction, every action, every decision made on a blockchain is recorded and publicly accessible. No edits, no backroom deals, no missing files. If the Department of Government Efficiency were running things, there would be no hiding mismanaged funds, no mysteriously over-budget defense projects, no tax loopholes buried in thousands of pages of legal jargon. Every dollar spent, every vote cast, every government contract awarded—visible, verifiable, impossible to alter.

For anyone who has ever doubted government accountability, it sounds like a dream. A government without corruption, inefficiency, or waste, running on code instead of career politicians with ulterior motives. Instead of politicians deciding which programs get funded based on backroom negotiations, smart contracts could automate spending based on preset rules. No lobbying. No pork-barrel projects. No billion-dollar bridges to nowhere.

But that's the optimistic version.

The other possibility is that a blockchain-powered government wouldn't just eliminate inefficiency—it would eliminate privacy. A perfect record of every financial transaction? That's great when you're tracking fraud, but not so great when you're a private citizen who doesn't want the government monitoring every dollar you spend. A voting system where every ballot is counted instantly? Fantastic—unless it means an end to anonymous voting, replaced with a system where political opinions are permanently tied to digital identities.

What happens when the technology meant to keep governments honest becomes a tool for total oversight? A system that can track every tax dollar can also track every purchase. A system that ensures fair elections can also be used to permanently link every citizen to their political leanings. The same blockchain technology that can protect people from corruption can also be used to create a financial and legal record that follows them forever.

The problem isn't whether DOGE—or any blockchain-based government system—could work. The problem is who gets to control it. If the government builds the system, they set the rules. If private companies get involved, they become the gatekeepers of digital governance. If the public demands control, then you're talking about decentralized governance, which sounds good in theory but raises its own set of issues—who writes the code? Who decides when it changes? What happens when a flaw is discovered that needs to be fixed?

There's a reason governments move slowly. Bureaucracy, for all its flaws, is a form of control, designed to prevent drastic, immediate shifts in power. A blockchain-based government would be fast, efficient, and immune to manipulation—but only if it was built perfectly from day one. Otherwise, it would be the most effective tool of government overreach ever created, with no human element left to slow it down.

This is the paradox of technological progress. The more transparent systems become, the more power they hold. The real question isn't whether DOGE could work—it's whether anyone should want it to.

Chapter 6: The Role of AI & Automation in Government

Can AI Make Government More Efficient?

The idea of an AI-run government sounds like something out of a dystopian sci-fi movie. A world where cold, unfeeling algorithms make policy decisions, balance budgets, and approve or deny government aid with a precision that no human bureaucracy could match. But for all the fear that AI might turn governance into an emotionless, machine-driven nightmare, there's also an undeniable appeal.

Government, in its current form, is a slow-moving beast. It takes months, sometimes years, to pass legislation, approve infrastructure projects, or roll out new public services. Red tape is everywhere. Agencies are bogged down by inefficiencies, outdated technology, and layers of bureaucracy that exist more to preserve power than to get things done. If AI could streamline even a fraction of that process, it would represent one of the most significant shifts in governance since the invention of democracy itself.

The potential is staggering. AI could analyze massive amounts of data in real time, identifying wasteful spending, optimizing public services, and even predicting future economic downturns before they happen. Imagine a government that could instantly process tax returns, approve business permits in seconds, and detect fraud before it even occurs. Instead of lawmakers fighting over budgets based on guesswork and political maneuvering, AI could allocate resources based on hard data, ensuring that taxpayer money is spent where it's actually needed.

In theory, an AI-powered government could make politics obsolete. If decisions were based purely on efficiency, rather than ideology, there would be no need for endless debates, filibusters, or partisan gridlock. Policy could be optimized like an algorithm—constantly learning, adapting, and improving without human interference.

But that's the theory. The reality is more complicated.

For AI to run government systems, it would need access to an unprecedented amount of data. That means more surveillance, more tracking, and more control over people's lives than any government has ever had before.

Every welfare check, every tax refund, every permit, every public service would be managed by algorithms—rules written by programmers who may or may not have the public's best interests in mind.

And then there's the bias problem. AI isn't neutral. It learns from data, and if that data is flawed, the AI will be flawed too. If a government AI is trained on years of discriminatory practices, it won't suddenly become fair—it will just automate injustice faster than ever before. An AI-driven welfare system could deny assistance to people based on patterns it doesn't fully understand. An AI-driven law enforcement system could reinforce racial and economic biases, turning predictive policing into a self-fulfilling prophecy.

There's also the question of accountability. When a government agency makes a mistake, there's a human being—an official, a lawmaker, a judge—who can be held responsible. If an AI system denies someone a business license, or wrongfully rejects a tax refund, who do they appeal to? Who takes the blame when the algorithm fails?

The answer probably isn't to remove humans from government entirely, but to find a way to merge

AI-driven efficiency with human oversight. The best version of AI in government wouldn't replace decision-makers—it would assist them, providing real-time analysis, automating the most mundane bureaucratic tasks, and ensuring that policies are based on facts rather than emotions.

If used correctly, AI could make government faster, smarter, and less wasteful. It could eliminate paperwork, reduce corruption, and ensure public funds are spent effectively. But if handed too much control, it could turn into the ultimate surveillance tool—efficient, unfeeling, and impossible to challenge.

AI isn't going to replace government tomorrow, but it's already working its way in. The question is whether we use it to make government better—or just more powerful.

Risks of Automating Governance

There's something seductive about the idea of a fully automated government. No more corruption, no more inefficiency, no more waiting in line at the DMV while a clerk manually types your information into an outdated database. AI doesn't take bribes. Blockchain doesn't lose paperwork. Algorithms don't waste tax dollars on pet projects designed to win elections rather than solve problems.

But the moment you take humans out of governance, things start to get complicated.

The biggest risk is that automation doesn't eliminate bias—it just makes it harder to fight. When a human bureaucrat makes a bad decision, you can appeal it. When an algorithm does, you're stuck arguing with lines of code. A perfectly efficient AI might determine that certain neighborhoods are at higher risk for crime and automatically allocate more police resources there. Sounds smart—except if that decision is based on flawed historical data, it could reinforce systemic bias, leading to a self-fulfilling prophecy where certain communities are permanently over-policed based on numbers, not reality.

Then there's the issue of control. Who programs the system? Who decides how policies are written into code? Imagine an AI-driven welfare system that automatically determines who qualifies for assistance. It might be more efficient than the current bureaucratic mess, but what happens when it starts denying people based on a technicality? Who do they call? What if it makes a mistake, but there's no human oversight to catch it? The more decisions we turn over to machines, the more we lose the ability to push back.

Even something as seemingly simple as tax collection becomes a potential minefield. If an AI system is designed to maximize efficiency, what's stopping it from automatically pulling money from your account the second you owe it? No delays, no appeals—just cold, hard automation. That's great if you trust the system. It's terrifying if you don't.

Automation also makes government harder to challenge. Right now, laws can be debated, rewritten, and overturned by elected officials. But what happens when policies are locked into smart contracts on a blockchain, designed to execute without human interference? If the code is wrong, who fixes it? If people don't like a policy, how do they change it? Democracy works, for better or worse, because it's messy. When you replace human judgment with automated rules, you might get efficiency—but you might also get a system that's impossible to break free from.

And that's where the real danger lies. Once governance becomes fully automated, turning back isn't easy. AI-driven systems don't retire. Blockchain-based laws don't just disappear. There's no one to vote out, no simple way to overhaul a system that's running exactly as it was programmed to. If the government becomes a machine, then the people it governs become little more than data points in an equation.

Technology has the power to make government faster, smarter, and more effective. But it also has the power to make it unaccountable, untouchable, and immune to change. The real risk of automating governance isn't that the system fails—it's that it works exactly as intended, and there's nothing anyone can do about it.

Who Controls the Algorithms?

At some point, the world stopped questioning whether AI and automation were going to run things and started asking a different question: who gets to control them? Because while the idea of a machine-driven, corruption-free government might sound appealing, the reality is that these systems don't exist in a vacuum. Somebody writes the code. Somebody decides what the algorithm prioritizes. And somebody stands to benefit.

Governments have always been about control. In the past, that control came through laws, enforcement, and the financial system. But in an era where algorithms dictate everything from search results to stock market movements, control isn't just about policy—it's about who gets to program the decision-making machines.

The people writing these algorithms aren't elected officials. They're not accountable to voters. They're engineers, data scientists, and private corporations operating in an opaque world where a few lines of code can dictate everything from who qualifies for a home loan to which neighborhoods get police patrols. These aren't traditional lawmakers, yet they're shaping the future of governance in ways most people don't even realize.

Take the financial system. High-frequency trading firms already use algorithms to make decisions in milliseconds, executing trades faster than any human ever could. Some of these firms control billions of dollars, and their AI models determine market movements. The average investor has no idea how these algorithms work, and there's no real oversight. Now imagine a government that functions the same way—where AI determines who receives benefits, how public funds are allocated, and which policies get prioritized. If you're on the winning side of that equation, you might never question it. But if you're on the losing side, what recourse do you have?

Then there's Big Tech. Google, Facebook, Amazon—these companies already influence public perception more than any government agency ever could. They determine what information people see, what products they buy, and even how they interact with political ideas. Their algorithms aren't just shaping individual choices; they're shaping society. And if these companies end up playing a major role in automating governance—whether through AI-driven policy implementation, digital identification systems, or blockchain-based financial tracking—the question of control becomes even more critical.

The biggest illusion about AI is that it's neutral. It isn't. AI models are built by humans, trained on data that reflects human biases, and optimized for objectives set by the people in charge. A government-run entirely on automation wouldn't be free of corruption—it would just be programmed to serve the interests of whoever designed it. If a corporation builds the system, they'll build it to protect profits. If a government agency builds it, they'll build it to preserve power.

And once an algorithm is in place, it doesn't easily change. Unlike human lawmakers who can be voted out, algorithms don't respond to public pressure. They don't adjust their priorities because of protests. If an AI-driven system is unfair, it doesn't fix itself—it just keeps running, executing rules exactly as it was designed to, with no consideration for the people caught in the crossfire.

If governance is going to be automated, transparency isn't optional—it's the only thing that matters. Who writes the code? Who audits the system? Who has the power to make changes? If the answer to those questions isn't clear, then it's not really governance anymore. It's just control, hidden behind a screen.

Chapter 7: Public Concerns & Controversies

Is This Just Another Bureaucratic Nightmare?

For all the talk about efficiency, automation, and a government run by algorithms, there's one question no one can seem to escape: isn't this just another bureaucratic nightmare waiting to happen?

Government inefficiency isn't just about outdated systems or sluggish decision-making. It's about layers upon layers of process, each one designed to prevent mistakes but ultimately creating a tangled mess of rules, forms, and delays. People already struggle to navigate basic government functions—getting a permit, applying for benefits, filing taxes—so what happens when you replace the slow-moving bureaucrat behind the desk with an unyielding algorithm?

The risk isn't just that an AI-driven system will fail—it's that it will fail in a way no one can fix. Bureaucracy, for all its flaws, still has human flexibility. If a caseworker sees an obvious mistake, they can override it. If a judge realizes a rule is unfair in practice, they can set a precedent to change it. But algorithms don't have that kind of discretion. They follow code. They apply rules exactly as they are written. There's no wiggle room, no exceptions, no sympathy for a unique situation.

Imagine applying for a business license through an automated system that denies you instantly because of a data mismatch. No explanation, no phone number to call, no appeal process beyond a cold, automated FAQ page. Or worse, imagine being flagged by an AI-driven fraud detection program that mistakenly locks you out of your own bank account. How do you argue with an algorithm? Who do you even talk to?

The nightmare scenario isn't some dystopian future where machines take over. It's a government that becomes so dependent on automation that it loses the ability to correct itself. A bureaucracy where mistakes don't get fixed because no one is left to question them.

Then there's the question of implementation. Governments have a track record of rolling out new technology in the most inefficient way possible. The Affordable Care Act website crashed on launch. State unemployment systems during the pandemic collapsed under the weight of digital traffic. Even the IRS struggles to update its decades-old software. If agencies can't handle basic web portals without turning them into logistical nightmares, how are they supposed to manage AI-driven governance?

The irony of a Department of Government Efficiency (DOGE) is that it could end up creating more inefficiency. Every new system needs maintenance, oversight, and updates. Every algorithm needs auditing. And because government contracts tend to go to the slowest-moving, highest-bidding firms, there's a real chance that an AI-powered bureaucracy would be just as bloated and dysfunctional as the human-driven one—just with more complicated error messages.

The real question isn't whether automation can improve governance. It's whether it can do so without making things worse. If it creates a system that's harder to navigate, more frustrating to interact with, and impossible to challenge, then it's not really efficiency—it's just bureaucracy, dressed up in better technology.

Government Efficiency vs. Government Control

There's a thin line between making something more efficient and making it more powerful. The same technology that speeds things up, removes bottlenecks, and eliminates waste also consolidates control. The question isn't whether AI and automation can make government run better—it's what happens when they do.

For most of history, government inefficiency has been its own kind of safeguard. A slow-moving bureaucracy means no single person or institution can change the system overnight. Politicians can push policies, but they have to fight through layers of approval, legal challenges, and public debate. The wheels turn slowly, but that slowness prevents abuse.

Now, imagine a government that operates at the speed of an algorithm. Public services delivered instantly. Tax returns processed in seconds. Welfare applications approved—or denied—without human involvement. The inefficiencies are gone, but so are the barriers that once kept power in check.

Efficiency sounds good until you realize it also makes control easier. A government that can instantly approve a business license can just as easily revoke one. A tax system that automatically deducts what you owe can also freeze your assets with no warning. AI-driven law enforcement can catch criminals faster, but it can also flag innocent people with no clear way to appeal.

The more efficient a system becomes, the harder it is to resist. When bureaucracy is slow, people have time to push back. They can organize, challenge unfair rulings, demand new policies. But when governance is automated, the response time shrinks. The government makes a decision, and it executes instantly—no delays, no debates, no human discretion.

This isn't some far-off dystopian scenario. China's social credit system already operates on a version of this model. Citizens are scored based on their behavior—paying bills on time, following laws, supporting government policies. A high score gets you perks like cheaper loans and travel privileges. A low score means restrictions, from financial penalties to being barred from certain services. It's efficient, but it's also total control wrapped in the language of optimization.

The U.S. isn't China, but the technology is already here. AI systems track financial transactions, flagging unusual behavior for potential fraud. Automated content moderation determines what can and can't be said online. Government agencies already use predictive analytics to determine who qualifies for benefits, who is at risk of defaulting on loans, and who should be monitored for criminal activity.

The problem isn't the technology—it's who decides how it's used. Efficiency in government isn't inherently bad. Reducing waste, cutting through red tape, making services more accessible—those are all good things. But when efficiency removes the human element, when it turns governance into a machine that can't be questioned, that's when it stops being about making things better and starts being about control.

A government that's too slow is frustrating. A government that's too fast is dangerous. Somewhere between inefficiency and automation is a balance, but finding it won't be easy. Because once a system is built for efficiency, it doesn't take much to turn it into something else entirely.

How It Might Affect Your Daily Life

For most people, government efficiency—or inefficiency—is something they only think about when they have to. You don't wake up wondering about the bureaucratic machinery that processes your taxes, issues your driver's license, or determines the zoning laws in your neighborhood. You only notice it when it slows you down—when you're stuck on hold with the DMV, waiting weeks for a permit, or wading through confusing paperwork for a loan application.

But what happens when all of that changes? What does a government run by AI and automation actually look like in your daily life?

It starts small. You renew your passport without filling out a form—because the system already knows your information and processes it automatically. A government AI flags a pothole on your street through satellite data and schedules a repair before you even call to complain. Your tax refund hits your bank account the same day you file. At first, it feels like magic—like someone finally fixed the system.

Then, one day, you apply for a mortgage and get denied instantly. No explanation, no human to call—just an automated decision based on an algorithm that's seen something in your financial history that makes you a risk. Maybe it's a pattern it picked up that you don't even recognize. Maybe it's wrong. Either way, it's not a loan officer making the call—it's a system running millions of calculations in the background.

You get a speeding ticket in the mail, but there was no cop involved. A network of traffic cameras and AI sensors caught you, clocked your speed, and issued the fine before you even got home. There's no arguing, no plea for leniency—the system doesn't care if you were trying to avoid an accident or rushing to the hospital. The numbers say you were speeding, so you were.

You try to start a small business. Instead of filling out paperwork and waiting weeks for approval, you're assigned a business ID instantly. It's all digital, tracked on a blockchain system that keeps your licenses, tax filings, and financial records in one place. No accountants, no lost documents. But then you realize the same system is monitoring every transaction you make. The moment a government AI detects something suspicious—too much cash flow in one direction, a mismatch between your reported earnings and your expenses—you're flagged. Maybe it's nothing. Maybe it's an audit. Maybe it's something worse.

And it's not just money. AI-driven healthcare systems might determine your eligibility for medical procedures based on risk calculations, not doctor recommendations. AI-powered law enforcement could predict crimes before they happen, assigning police presence to areas based on data patterns rather than human judgment. Public assistance programs might determine how much support you qualify for, not based on a caseworker's understanding of your situation, but on a cold equation that factors in your digital footprint.

At first, all of this feels like efficiency. Services work better, paperwork disappears, government functions like a streamlined business. But the more automated the system becomes, the less room there is for exceptions, for nuance, for humanity. You don't talk to people anymore—you talk to algorithms. The government isn't slow anymore, but it's also not something you can question. Decisions happen in an instant, and they feel final because, in many cases, they are.

Most people won't notice the change immediately. It will feel like progress. But the moment you find yourself on the wrong side of an algorithm, when the system decides something about you that you can't appeal, can't argue, can't even understand—that's when you'll realize the cost of perfect efficiency.

Part 3: The Bigger Picture – The Intersection of Technology, Finance & Government

Chapter 8: Elon Musk, Crypto, & Government Disruption

Musk's Vision for the Future of Finance & Government

Elon Musk doesn't just predict the future—he forces it into existence. He's done it with electric cars, with reusable rockets, with AI, and even with a tunnel-boring machine that may or may not ever solve traffic congestion. But one of his most unpredictable disruptions has been in finance and government—two systems that weren't exactly looking for disruption in the first place.

Musk isn't a banker. He isn't a politician. He isn't a traditional economist. But that's exactly what makes him dangerous to those industries. He doesn't play by their rules, and more importantly, he doesn't care about their rules. When he started pushing Dogecoin as the "people's crypto," it wasn't because he believed in its economic model or thought it would replace the U.S. dollar. He saw something else: the power of decentralized, internet-driven finance to shake up a system that had been running the same way for centuries.

Musk has always had a libertarian streak when it comes to money. He's talked openly about how central banks manipulate currencies, how inflation erodes the value of hard work, and how government regulation slows down innovation. His companies—Tesla, SpaceX, and even Twitter (now X)—all operate with a philosophy of breaking barriers, whether it's launching a car into orbit or making people pay for blue checkmarks. He looks at crypto and sees the same thing: a way to take power away from centralized institutions and put it in the hands of the people.

But Musk's version of the future isn't just about decentralized money. It's about an entirely new way of running things—one where AI, blockchain, and automation replace bureaucracy, where government is streamlined to the point of being nearly invisible, where finance is frictionless and global. In his mind, everything from business licenses to voting systems could be handled through technology, making government less of a monolithic force and more of a background service—there when you need it, otherwise out of the way.

It sounds like a utopian vision—until you realize how much control it requires. Musk might be against traditional government overreach, but his companies operate in highly centralized ways. Tesla doesn't have a democratic process for decision-making; Musk decides, and things happen. SpaceX doesn't debate whether or not to launch a rocket; Musk sets the goal, and his engineers execute. Even Twitter, the supposed bastion of free speech under his leadership, is ultimately dictated by his whims.

So what happens when a Musk-led vision for finance and government collides with reality? If Dogecoin—or any decentralized digital currency—becomes mainstream, it threatens the very foundations of government-controlled money. If AI-driven governance eliminates inefficiency, it also eliminates human discretion. If automation replaces government bureaucracy, it doesn't just remove red tape—it removes the people who challenge the system when it fails.

Musk sees himself as an architect of the future, but his visions always come with an implicit warning: be careful what you automate. When you build a system that's too efficient, too fast, too absolute, it can't be stopped once it's in motion. The financial system, the government, the very structure of society—they're all ripe for disruption. The only question is whether Musk's vision leads to more freedom or a world that moves so fast that nobody—not even him—can control it.

Why He Supports Crypto but Criticizes Bureaucracy

To understand why Elon Musk supports crypto while taking every opportunity to criticize government bureaucracy, you have to start with how he sees the world. Musk doesn't think in terms of institutions—he thinks in terms of systems. Governments, banks, and corporations are just outdated operating systems that run the world, full of inefficiencies, unnecessary rules, and middlemen who slow things down. Crypto, on the other hand, is a system that runs itself. No politicians, no paperwork, no waiting for approvals—just code executing exactly as it was designed to.

Musk has always been obsessed with efficiency. Tesla's production lines are designed to be as automated as possible. SpaceX's rockets are built with a singular goal: reduce costs and increase reusability. Even his Twitter (or X) takeover was about stripping away what he saw as unnecessary layers of moderation and verification. To Musk, crypto fits this mindset perfectly. It's money without borders, without a central authority, without the kind of bureaucracy that turns a simple financial transaction into a maze of regulations and fees.

He's not wrong about bureaucracy being inefficient. Governments move slowly because they were designed that way. Rules, committees, approval processes—these things exist to prevent corruption, but they also create a system where even the simplest tasks take forever. Want to start a business? You have to apply for permits, licenses, and approvals, each one requiring paperwork, fees, and wait times. Need to transfer money internationally? You're dealing with banks, compliance checks, and hidden fees that take days to process. Crypto removes all of that. Send money instantly, to anyone, anywhere, with no oversight.

That's why Musk loves it. But it's also why governments don't.

A world where crypto replaces traditional finance is a world where governments lose control over money. No more printing dollars to combat inflation. No more tracking every financial transaction for tax purposes. No more using financial policy as a tool to shape the economy. Musk sees that as a feature, not a bug. He believes that money should be like the internet—decentralized, open-source, and resistant to censorship. Governments, of course, see it differently.

That's where his criticism of bureaucracy comes in. Musk doesn't just dislike inefficiency—he sees it as an existential threat to progress. He believes red tape and regulation slow down innovation, preventing bold ideas from becoming reality. SpaceX had to fight through years of regulatory approvals just to launch rockets. Tesla faced resistance from auto dealerships and unions trying to protect the traditional car industry. Every new technology he pushes runs into the same wall of government inertia.

Crypto, in Musk's eyes, is the perfect rebellion. It's innovation that governments can't fully control, a financial system that exists outside their reach. It's the same reason he's fascinated by artificial intelligence and brain-computer interfaces—systems that bypass traditional power structures and create entirely new ways of operating.

But here's the contradiction: for all his talk of decentralization, Musk himself runs highly centralized companies. Tesla, SpaceX, Neuralink—these aren't democracies. They're led by him, with decision-making concentrated in his hands. He believes in efficiency, but only when he's the one setting the direction. He hates government red tape, but he also wants the power to shape the future without interference.

That's why his support for crypto makes sense, but his vision for replacing bureaucracy is more complicated. A world without bureaucrats sounds great until you realize that rules and oversight exist for a reason. If everything runs on AI, automation, and blockchain, what happens when the system fails? Who do you appeal to when an algorithm decides you don't qualify for a loan, a medical procedure, or a business permit?

Musk wants a world where technology replaces inefficiency, where crypto replaces traditional finance, where governments don't slow things down. But what he hasn't fully answered is what happens when that system—his system—becomes the new bureaucracy, just faster, more automated, and harder to challenge.

Could a Private Citizen Like Musk Run a More Efficient Government?

Elon Musk already runs multiple companies that operate like miniature governments. Tesla isn't just a car company—it's an energy provider, a robotics lab, and a manufacturing empire rolled into one. SpaceX has its own rules, its own security, even its own space program. And Twitter—now X—became his personal experiment in rewriting the rules of digital communication. If you look at how Musk operates, he doesn't see institutions as fixed entities. He sees them as inefficient systems in need of an upgrade.

So could someone like Musk—someone outside the political establishment, with unlimited resources and a tech-first mindset—actually run a more efficient government?

The appeal is obvious. Governments are slow, bloated, and resistant to change. Private companies, especially ones led by visionaries, move fast. They innovate, disrupt, and cut through bureaucracy like a knife through butter. A government designed by Musk wouldn't waste years debating infrastructure bills—it would just build the damn roads, using AI-driven logistics to optimize every detail. It wouldn't get stuck in endless committee hearings—it would make decisions in real time, based on live data. Efficiency would replace tradition, and technology would replace paperwork.

But efficiency isn't the same as good governance. Musk's companies are efficient because they don't answer to millions of people with different needs, opinions, and expectations. They answer to him. Tesla employees don't vote on company policy. SpaceX engineers don't hold town hall meetings to debate the ethics of a Mars colony. When Musk decides something, it happens.

Government, on the other hand, isn't supposed to be efficient—it's supposed to be accountable. The reason policies take time to pass, the reason regulations exist, the reason bureaucracy moves at a crawl is because governments are built to serve millions of people with competing interests. A healthcare system that works for one group might fail another. A tax policy that boosts economic growth might widen income inequality. In a democracy, the trade-offs have to be debated, not dictated.

That's the biggest flaw in the idea of a CEO-style government. Efficiency means making fast decisions, but fast decisions don't always serve the people they affect. Governments aren't inefficient because they want to be—they're inefficient because they have to balance power, rights, and responsibilities in a way that no private company ever does.

Even Musk, for all his obsession with speed and disruption, runs into this problem. Tesla has faced lawsuits over worker conditions. SpaceX has battled regulators over safety concerns. His attempt to overhaul Twitter in a matter of months led to mass layoffs, platform instability, and an advertising exodus. Speed and efficiency are great in theory, but in practice, they can create as many problems as they solve.

Still, the idea of a privately-run government isn't going away. Tech billionaires have already started funding experiments in alternative governance—charter cities, seasteading communities, blockchain-based economies that operate outside traditional nation-states. The dream is a system that moves as fast as a startup, where policies adapt in real time, where bureaucracy is reduced to a few lines of code.

But the moment you remove democratic oversight, the moment you replace elected officials with an unelected executive making all the calls, you've built something different. Not a government—an empire. It might be efficient. It might be innovative. It might even work. But it won't be a democracy, and it won't be built to serve everyone.

Musk could run a more efficient government. The real question is whether anyone should want him to.

Chapter 9: The War on Cash & The Rise of Digital Currency

How Governments are Moving Towards a Cashless Society

If you've been paying attention, cash is already on its way out. Fewer people carry bills in their wallets. Stores are adding signs that say "Card Only." Even places like Starbucks and McDonald's, where cash was once king, now push mobile payments first.

Governments have noticed. And they're not just watching the transition—they're accelerating it.

A cashless society isn't just about convenience. It's about control. When people use cash, transactions are anonymous. No digital footprint, no centralized ledger, no easy way to track who's spending what and where. But when everything moves to digital currency—credit cards, mobile payments, central bank digital currencies (CBDCs)—every transaction becomes part of a data stream, stored, analyzed, and, in some cases, regulated.

Governments aren't banning cash outright, but they don't have to. The push toward digital payments is happening naturally, driven by technology, consumer habits, and corporate interests. Every time a major retailer stops accepting cash, every time a bank charges a fee for withdrawing paper money, every time a financial app makes it easier to send payments with a tap, cash becomes less relevant.

The pandemic sped up the shift. Businesses that once accepted cash suddenly refused it, citing health concerns. Contactless payments surged, and companies like Apple Pay, Venmo, and PayPal saw their usage skyrocket. Once people got used to tapping their phones instead of pulling out bills, there was no going back.

But this isn't just about credit cards and mobile wallets. Governments are going further. The U.S., China, the European Union—nearly every major economic power is developing or piloting a central bank digital currency. A CBDC is different from traditional digital payments because it's not just electronic money—it's government-issued, fully programmable, and directly linked to the financial system.

China is already ahead of the curve. The country's digital yuan, or e-CNY, is being rolled out in cities across the country. Unlike Bitcoin or decentralized cryptocurrencies, the digital yuan is fully controlled by China's central bank. It can be tracked, restricted, or even programmed to expire after a certain period. The government has the ability to see every transaction in real time, freeze accounts instantly, or even prevent money from being spent on specific goods or services.

The U.S. has been more cautious, but the Federal Reserve has been researching its own digital dollar for years. In theory, a digital dollar could make transactions faster, reduce banking fees, and streamline government payments like stimulus checks and tax refunds. But it also raises concerns about surveillance, privacy, and financial control.

The advantages of a cashless society are obvious. Digital payments are faster, more secure, and easier to integrate with global markets. Governments argue that eliminating cash would reduce crime, make tax evasion harder, and prevent money laundering. But the downside is just as clear. A fully digital financial system means no off-grid transactions, no financial privacy, and no way to function without approval from the banking system.

What happens if the government decides to freeze accounts during a crisis? What if certain purchases are restricted by policy? What if an algorithm flags your transactions as suspicious, and suddenly your money stops working?

Cash may seem old-fashioned, but it still represents financial freedom. A world without it might be more efficient, but it will also be one where every transaction is monitored, every dollar is traceable, and financial independence is something granted—not assumed.

Are CBDCs (Central Bank Digital Currencies) a Threat to Crypto?

Crypto was built to escape the financial system. Bitcoin wasn't designed to work alongside banks—it was designed to replace them. The whole point of decentralized currency was to take power away from central authorities, to give people a way to store and transfer value without oversight, without permission, without middlemen.

CBDCs—the digital currencies being developed by central banks around the world—are the exact opposite. They take everything crypto was trying to avoid and bake it directly into the system. These aren't decentralized assets running on public blockchains. They are fully controlled, programmable, and tied to national economies in a way that makes them feel less like an evolution of money and more like an upgraded surveillance tool.

That's why crypto purists see them as a direct threat.

Governments won't come out and say they're trying to kill decentralized crypto, but they don't have to. If they create a digital currency that's easy to use, integrated with banks, and backed by the full faith of a nation's economy, they don't need to ban Bitcoin or Ethereum—they just need to make them irrelevant. The average person isn't going to jump through hoops to use decentralized crypto when a CBDC is seamlessly built into their financial life. If your employer pays you in digital dollars, if your rent, taxes, and bills can be automatically deducted, if every store accepts it without friction—why bother with Bitcoin?

That's the long game. Governments don't need to outlaw crypto to weaken it. They just have to offer something more convenient, more stable, and more embedded in daily life. And once they do that, they can start phasing out cash, tightening regulations on private cryptocurrencies, and shifting people into a system where every financial transaction is tracked, monitored, and—if necessary—restricted.

Crypto enthusiasts argue that true decentralization will always be valuable. That people who care about financial privacy, censorship resistance, and autonomy will continue to use Bitcoin, Ethereum, and other decentralized networks, no matter how seamless CBDCs become. And they might be right—there will always be a subset of people who don't trust governments with their money.

But for the masses? Convenience always wins.

CBDCs won't kill crypto outright, but they could push it further to the fringes. Instead of being a mainstream alternative to banks, crypto might become a niche tool for those who want to operate outside the system—a digital parallel to cash, used in ways that aren't always welcomed by regulators.

In the end, it's not just a fight over money. It's a fight over control. Crypto represents financial independence. CBDCs represent government oversight. The battle isn't about which technology is better—it's about who gets to decide how money works in the digital age. And governments aren't about to let that power slip away without a fight.

What Happens if the U.S. Adopts a Digital Dollar?

At first, nothing would seem different. You'd still get paid, still pay bills, still buy coffee with the same debit card or phone app. But underneath it all, the financial system would be running on something entirely new—money that exists only in digital form, issued directly by the Federal Reserve, replacing paper dollars with code.

A digital dollar wouldn't be just another payment method. It wouldn't be like Venmo, PayPal, or a bank transfer. It would be money without a middleman. Right now, when you swipe a credit card or send money through an app, banks process the transaction, acting as intermediaries. A central bank digital currency (CBDC) would cut them out. The U.S. government would have the ability to issue, track, and manage money directly. No third parties, no lag, no fees.

That kind of efficiency sounds great—until you realize what else it enables.

A digital dollar means every transaction is recorded on a centralized ledger, monitored in real time. Tax collection becomes automatic. Illegal transactions become nearly impossible. Financial fraud is reduced. On paper, these are all positives. But they also mean privacy disappears. With cash, you can buy something without leaving a trace. With a CBDC, every cent you spend is logged. Not necessarily by a shadowy government agent, but by an algorithm that flags anything unusual.

And that's where things get complicated.

If the U.S. fully transitions to a digital dollar, cash will inevitably disappear. It won't happen overnight, but as stores and banks move away from paper money, people will have little choice but to use the digital system. At that point, financial freedom isn't just about how much money you have—it's about whether you're allowed to use it.

A government-controlled digital currency could be programmed. That means restrictions can be placed on how money is spent. Stimulus checks could be issued with expiration dates, forcing people to spend rather than save. Welfare benefits could be limited to certain purchases, automatically rejecting anything outside approved categories. Sanctions on individuals—freezing assets, blocking purchases—could happen instantly, at the push of a button.

The Federal Reserve insists that any digital dollar would be designed to protect privacy, that it wouldn't be used to monitor or control individuals. But the reality is, once the infrastructure exists, it can be used however future governments see fit. Maybe one administration keeps the system neutral, but what about the next? What happens in a crisis, when financial restrictions are suddenly justified as a national security measure?

Even banks wouldn't be safe. If people could store digital dollars directly with the Federal Reserve, why would they need a traditional bank? The entire banking system relies on deposits—banks take in customer funds, lend them out, and make money on the spread. If those deposits start flowing directly to a government-issued digital wallet, banks lose their core function. They could adapt, shifting to investment and lending services, but the balance of power in finance would shift permanently.

And then there's the geopolitical angle. The U.S. dollar is the world's reserve currency, used in global trade and held by foreign governments as a safe asset. A digital dollar would speed up international transactions, making it easier to bypass the slow-moving network of banks and payment processors. That's great for efficiency, but it also creates a new battleground. Countries like China and Russia have already explored ways to move away from reliance on the U.S. dollar in global trade. A digital dollar could either strengthen America's financial dominance—or give other nations a reason to build competing systems.

For the average person, a digital dollar wouldn't feel revolutionary at first. It would be introduced gradually, probably as an option alongside traditional banking. But over time, it would become the default. And once that happens, financial independence changes forever. A world without cash is a world where every transaction is permissioned. That doesn't mean everyday life grinds to a halt—but it does mean the financial system becomes something you don't just participate in. It becomes something that can be switched off.

Chapter 10: The Future of Money, Governance, and Doge

Will Decentralization Win?

The battle between decentralization and central control isn't new. It's the same fight that's played out in politics, finance, and technology for centuries—individual freedom versus institutional power, personal autonomy versus systemic efficiency. The difference now is that technology has given both sides new weapons. Governments and financial institutions have never had more tools for surveillance and control, but at the same time, decentralized systems—crypto, blockchain, DAOs—have never had more potential to work outside of those traditional structures.

If decentralization is going to win, it's not going to be because Bitcoin or Dogecoin hits a certain price target. It's not even going to be because people suddenly rise up and reject government-controlled money. If it happens, it will be because decentralized systems become too useful, too frictionless, and too ingrained in daily life to ignore.

Right now, decentralization is still a choice. You have to opt into it. Buying crypto requires an active decision to step outside traditional banking. Using DeFi means understanding a new set of financial rules, taking on risk, and trusting a system that isn't backed by institutions. For decentralization to win, it has to stop being an alternative and start being the default.

That means more than just crypto adoption—it means decentralized infrastructure for everything. Payment systems that don't rely on banks. Governance models that don't depend on elected officials. Digital identities that aren't tied to government databases. The dream isn't just a world where money is decentralized; it's a world where power is.

But decentralization also has its own flaws. It's chaotic. It's vulnerable to manipulation in different ways—scams, hacks, power struggles within leaderless systems. Governments move slowly because they're designed to prevent sudden shifts in power. Decentralized systems move at the speed of the internet, and sometimes, that's too fast for their own good.

Look at the early days of crypto. Exchanges collapsed overnight. ICO scams stole billions. Entire blockchain networks rose and fell within months. Even today, decentralized finance is a Wild West, full of opportunities but also full of risks. The same lack of oversight that makes it powerful also makes it fragile.

So the real question isn't whether decentralization will win—it's whether it will mature fast enough to survive its own volatility. Will it stabilize before governments figure out how to regulate or replace it? Will people trust it enough to rely on it for something as fundamental as money?

Dogecoin, in its own strange way, represents both the promise and the absurdity of decentralization. It was never meant to be a serious financial tool, and yet it became one. Not because it was the most advanced cryptocurrency, but because people wanted it to exist. It proved that money, at its core, is just a shared belief system. If enough people decide that something has value, it does.

That's the real power of decentralization. It's not about technology—it's about belief. If people believe in a system enough to use it, to build on it, to defend it, then it becomes real. If they don't, it disappears.

Governments, banks, and institutions aren't going to voluntarily give up control. If decentralization wins, it won't be because of a single breakthrough or a sudden shift. It will be because people, over time, choose systems that give them more autonomy. It will be because decentralized tools become more useful than centralized ones. It will be because the friction of dealing with bureaucracy, banks, and regulations finally outweighs the risks of trusting code over institutions.

The future of money, governance, and even Dogecoin isn't going to be decided by policy papers or corporate boardrooms. It's going to be decided the way all major shifts in history have been—by what people choose to use, what they're willing to trust, and whether they're ready to bet on a system that, for all its flaws, gives them more control over their own lives.

Could We See a Government-Sanctioned Meme Currency?

It sounds ridiculous—too absurd even for a world where Dogecoin once hit an $80 billion market cap. A government-backed meme currency? A financial system built not on gold reserves or economic output, but on internet culture, viral momentum, and collective belief? Yet, when you step back and look at how money actually works, it starts to seem less like a joke and more like an inevitability.

Because at the end of the day, money is already a meme. The U.S. dollar holds value not because of anything tangible, but because people believe it does. Bitcoin's rise wasn't built on utility alone—it was built on a narrative, a story about decentralized money taking power from governments. Dogecoin, for all its absurdity, thrived because people saw it as a rebellion against traditional finance.

If belief is what gives money power, why wouldn't governments try to harness that?

It wouldn't happen overnight. Governments don't move fast, and they certainly don't embrace disruption unless they're forced to. But they also don't ignore trends that threaten their control. If a meme currency gains enough traction—if it becomes widely accepted, deeply embedded in the economy, and seen as a legitimate store of value—governments will have two choices: regulate it to death or absorb it into the system.

The second option is more interesting.

Imagine the Federal Reserve launching "FedDoge," a government-backed meme currency designed to appeal to younger generations. It wouldn't replace the U.S. dollar, but it would serve as a parallel digital asset, something that could be used for payments, savings, or even stimulus programs. Unlike Bitcoin, it would have stability. Unlike Dogecoin, it would have legitimacy. It would be a hybrid—part joke, part serious financial instrument, fully controlled by the government but marketed like a viral brand.

A meme currency with institutional backing might sound absurd, but consider what's already happening. The European Central Bank and the Federal Reserve are both exploring digital currencies. Politicians are increasingly using internet culture as a tool for engagement. Entire movements—financial, political, and social—are being built on the back of memes. A government-sanctioned meme currency wouldn't be about financial necessity. It would be about influence. About keeping people inside a system rather than letting them drift toward something uncontrollable.

There's precedent for this kind of shift. During the rise of social media, traditional institutions initially dismissed it as trivial—something for entertainment, not serious business. Then they realized they had no choice but to engage with it, adapt to it, and eventually use it to their advantage. A government-backed meme currency could follow the same pattern. What starts as a joke becomes real because people believe in it. Once that belief is strong enough, institutions co-opt it, giving it structure while maintaining the illusion of freedom.

Would it work? Maybe. The internet moves fast, but institutions move slow. If governments try to manufacture a meme currency from scratch, it might flop—too corporate, too artificial, too obviously a tool of control. But if they find a way to tap into an existing movement, to give legitimacy to something already fueled by internet culture, it could change the financial system in ways we haven't even begun to imagine.

The real question isn't whether a government-backed meme currency could happen. It's whether, when it does, people will trust it—or whether they'll see it for what it really is: the establishment's attempt to turn rebellion into another line item on the balance sheet.

What You Can Do to Prepare for This Changing Landscape

For most people, financial change happens slowly. You don't wake up one morning to find that cash is gone, that your bank account has been replaced with a central bank digital currency, or that a government-sanctioned meme coin is suddenly legal tender. It happens in pieces—one store stops accepting cash, then another, then another. One by one, banks roll out new digital systems, making it easier to use them than not. Before you know it, you're fully in the new system, and you never made a conscious decision to get there.

That's how financial shifts work. Not with a dramatic announcement, but with slow, incremental change until one day you realize there's no going back. Which means if you want to be prepared for what's coming, you need to be ahead of that curve.

The first step is understanding where money is going. It's not just about crypto or cashless payments or government-controlled digital currencies—it's about all of them at once. The financial world is splintering.

Traditional banking isn't disappearing, but it's evolving. Crypto isn't replacing fiat currency, but it's becoming a parallel system that more people are using. The future of money won't be one thing—it'll be a mix of old and new, centralized and decentralized, corporate and independent.

The key is flexibility. Relying on only one system—whether it's traditional banks, crypto, or cash—is a risk. If governments fully adopt digital currencies, cash will become harder to use. If regulations tighten on crypto, decentralized assets could become more difficult to access. The smartest move isn't to go all-in on any single financial system, but to be ready to navigate all of them.

If you haven't already, learn how to use cryptocurrency. You don't need to become a hardcore trader, but understanding how to hold, transfer, and secure digital assets is no longer just for tech enthusiasts. Even if you never plan to go fully into crypto, having the option gives you financial flexibility.

At the same time, pay attention to how governments are rolling out digital currencies. If a central bank digital currency (CBDC) becomes the default in your country, understand what that means for privacy, for financial autonomy, for your ability to control your own money. If there are restrictions on how and where money can be spent, you need to know how to work within—or around—the system.

And don't overlook cash. It's easy to assume that because digital transactions are more convenient, cash is irrelevant. But cash still represents financial freedom in a way digital money doesn't. It's untraceable, immune to technical failures, and valuable in situations where digital systems go down. If a fully digital financial world makes you uneasy, keeping some cash on hand is a simple way to maintain a degree of control.

Then there's the bigger picture: the role of corporations and governments in shaping the financial landscape. If you're relying entirely on major tech platforms—whether for payments, banking, or even investing—realize that these companies have policies that can change overnight. They can restrict transactions, ban accounts, and enforce regulations that aren't necessarily laws but function like them. Diversifying where you store and move money, even within the digital world, can give you more independence.

None of this is about doomsday prepping. It's about being realistic. The financial system is changing, and the best way to protect yourself is to stay informed and adaptable. The people who get caught off guard aren't the ones who didn't see change coming—they're the ones who assumed it wouldn't affect them.

Conclusion: The Doge Revolution – A Movement or a Passing Trend?

Why These Topics Matter Now

It's easy to dismiss Dogecoin as a joke. In fact, that's exactly what it was designed to be. A playful rebellion against the self-serious world of cryptocurrency, a meme turned into money. And yet, somehow, it has lasted longer than many of the so-called "serious" financial innovations of the past decade.

But Dogecoin is bigger than Dogecoin. It's a symbol of a shift that's happening right now—a battle between traditional finance and decentralized alternatives, between government control and digital autonomy, between efficiency and oversight. Whether or not Dogecoin itself remains relevant in five or ten years, the ideas it represents aren't going away.

These topics matter now because the way we use money is changing faster than at any other time in modern history. Cash is disappearing. Central banks are experimenting with digital currencies that could redefine financial privacy and control. Cryptocurrency, once seen as a niche asset, is forcing its way into mainstream finance, even as governments try to regulate it into submission. At the same time, automation and AI are creeping into governance, raising questions about who—or what—will be making the decisions that shape society in the coming years.

This isn't just a financial shift. It's a power shift. Who controls money has always been at the heart of who controls the world. For centuries, that control has rested with governments and banks. But technology has introduced something new: the ability for money to exist outside of traditional systems, for people to transact without intermediaries, for financial power to be decentralized in ways that were never possible before.

The rise of meme currencies, the push for a cashless society, the government's interest in digital money—these aren't separate issues. They're all connected. They're all part of a larger story about how power, money, and influence are being reshaped in real time.

So is the Doge Revolution a movement or a passing trend?

The answer depends on how you define it. If you're asking whether Dogecoin will still be relevant in twenty years, nobody knows. It might fade into internet history, a relic of an era when people briefly believed that a Shiba Inu meme could be worth billions. Or it might evolve, finding new use cases, embedding itself into digital culture in ways that keep it alive far longer than anyone expected.

But if you're asking whether the ideas behind Dogecoin—the shift toward decentralized money, the rejection of traditional financial gatekeepers, the belief that value is whatever people decide it is—are here to stay, the answer is already clear.

The financial world is at an inflection point. The systems that have existed for centuries are being challenged, redefined, and in some cases, replaced. Whether that future leans toward decentralization or government-controlled digital currencies will depend on what people choose to use, what they're willing to trust, and how much control they're willing to give up in exchange for convenience.

Dogecoin, in all its absurdity, was a warning shot—a reminder that money, at its core, is just a shared belief. And in a world where belief moves faster than ever, the institutions that once held absolute power over finance are no longer the only ones writing the rules.

What to Watch for in the Next Few Years

The financial world is shifting faster than at any point in modern history. Money is no longer just something you keep in a wallet or a bank—it's an evolving concept, shaped by technology, government policy, and the unpredictable nature of the internet. Whether you're paying attention or not, the next few years will determine what the future of money looks like. If you want to stay ahead, here's what to watch.

The first battleground is **central bank digital currencies (CBDCs)**. Governments around the world are laying the groundwork for digital versions of their national currencies. The U.S. has been slow to commit, but the research is there. China, meanwhile, is already rolling out the digital yuan, a fully controlled, fully trackable alternative to cash. The key question is how much control these digital currencies will give governments over individual financial decisions. Will they be programmable, meaning they can expire or be restricted for certain uses? Will they phase out cash entirely? The moment a major country fully commits to a CBDC, the global financial system will never be the same.

Then there's **crypto regulation**. Right now, the crypto market is still in a gray area—too big to ignore, too decentralized to fully control. Governments don't like money existing outside their oversight, but banning crypto outright hasn't worked. Instead, regulators are trying to box it in with strict rules on exchanges, stablecoins, and decentralized finance (DeFi). The more barriers they put up, the harder it will be for crypto to function as an alternative to traditional finance. If regulation tightens too much, expect crypto to move further underground, operating in ways that governments can't easily track or stop.

Another major shift to watch is the **slow disappearance of cash**. Businesses are already phasing it out. Banks are making it harder to withdraw large amounts. The moment cash becomes too inconvenient to use, most people will stop using it. Once that happens, financial privacy changes forever. A cashless society means every transaction is traceable. It means governments, banks, and corporations can monitor—and potentially control—how people spend their money. The move away from cash won't be announced as an official policy; it will just happen, one step at a time, until it's too late to turn back.

Meanwhile, **artificial intelligence is creeping into finance and governance**. Algorithms already determine credit scores, detect fraud, and approve or deny loans. But as AI becomes more powerful, it won't just be influencing financial decisions—it will be making them. Governments will use AI to automate tax collection, social benefits, and even economic policy. The real danger isn't just efficiency—it's what happens when AI systems make mistakes, when they deny someone access to their own money, when there's no human oversight to correct bad decisions.

Then there's the wildcard: **corporations creating their own financial systems**. Apple, Amazon, and other tech giants already control massive portions of the financial infrastructure through payments, credit cards, and digital wallets. It's only a matter of time before one of them makes a serious move toward launching a corporate-backed currency or financial network that rivals traditional banking. If people trust a company like Apple more than their government, what happens when Apple starts offering financial services that bypass banks altogether?

And, of course, there's **the cultural shift around money itself**. Younger generations don't think about money the way their parents did. They're more comfortable with digital assets, with decentralized finance, with the idea that currency isn't necessarily tied to a government. If that mindset becomes dominant, the future of money won't be determined by central banks or policymakers—it will be determined by what people actually choose to use.

The next few years will decide which version of the future wins. Will financial power remain centralized, controlled by governments and major institutions? Or will decentralized systems, crypto, and alternative economies create a world where people have more control over their own money?

If history is any guide, the answer won't be clear until it's already happening. But by then, the rules of money will have changed—and the people who saw it coming will be the ones who are ready.

How to Stay Ahead of the Curve

When financial systems shift, most people don't realize it's happening until they're already in it. One day, cash is common; the next, stores start refusing it. One year, banks are the only option; the next, people are transferring money through decentralized apps with no middleman. These shifts don't happen with a single announcement—they happen gradually, then all at once. The only way to avoid being caught off guard is to see the signals before they become obvious.

The first step is to **pay attention to policy changes**. Governments don't wake up one morning and launch a fully digital currency. They test it, regulate the competition, create incentives for adoption, and—most importantly—frame the narrative in a way that makes it seem like the next logical step. If you wait until a central bank digital currency (CBDC) is fully implemented, it's too late to understand how it works or what your options are. The time to watch is now. Follow what the Federal Reserve, the European Central Bank, and other major financial institutions are saying. The language they use will tell you where they're headed.

At the same time, **understand decentralized alternatives**. Crypto isn't going anywhere, but it is evolving. Bitcoin isn't just an asset—it's a hedge against centralized financial control. Ethereum isn't just a blockchain—it's a framework for decentralized finance that could one day replace traditional banking. You don't need to be an investor, but you do need to know how these systems work. If CBDCs start limiting financial freedom, decentralized alternatives will be the escape valve. The people who know how to navigate them will have options; the people who don't will be stuck.

Be mindful of where and how you store money. Right now, banks still operate as the default, but that won't always be the case. If major financial shifts occur—whether through inflation, regulation, or technological disruption—you don't want to have all your assets trapped in a system that no longer works in your favor. Diversification isn't just about investing; it's about access. Digital wallets, hard assets, and alternative banking options could become critical in ways that seem unnecessary today.

Watch how businesses react. Governments may push for digital adoption, but companies drive it. If large retailers start phasing out cash, that's a sign. If major financial platforms integrate crypto without waiting for government approval, that's another. The private sector moves faster than regulation, and companies will always adopt the technologies that benefit them first. If you see them moving in a direction, assume the rest of the economy will follow.

Understand that **control and convenience are always traded together**. The easier a financial system is to use, the more oversight it typically comes with. A CBDC will make transactions faster, but it will also allow real-time tracking and restrictions. A centralized financial network will eliminate inefficiencies, but it will also remove privacy. The key is to recognize when convenience is becoming a trap. When the only way to function in the economy is through a single government-issued digital currency, it's no longer a choice—it's a requirement.

And finally, don't assume stability. The financial world is shifting beneath the surface. Some of these changes will make life easier; others will consolidate power in ways that aren't obvious until later. The people who stay ahead of the curve aren't just the ones who predict the future correctly—they're the ones who prepare for multiple possibilities. The world of money is changing, and the rules are being rewritten in real time. The question isn't whether it will affect you. It's whether you'll be ready when it does.

www.ingramcontent.com/pod-product-compliance
Lightning Source LLC
LaVergne TN
LVHW022228200926
848481LV00006B/2179
* 9 7 9 8 3 4 8 5 2 3 7 6 3 *